Feral Woman
Copyright © 2025 Aimee Hope

Original Cover Art by Vincent Macaluso

The font used is Calisto MT

Gnashing Teeth Publishing
242 East Main Street
Norman AR 71960
http://GnashingTeethPublishing.com

Printed in the United States of America

ISBN 978-1-966075-08-0

Non-Fiction: Poetry

Gnashing Teeth Publishing First Edition

Praise for *Feral Woman*

The Brotherhood is powerful. It has many members. They are of all
places. They are of all time. The members do not die. One is member
to the degree that he can be member, no more, no less, and that part
of him that is of the Brotherhood does not die.
From The Art Spirit by Robert Henri

In 2025 I met a Sister, Aimee Hope, a seed tossed by my poet
Brother, Burt Bradley. Together he and I taught students to see,
through writing and drawing. From over 30 years and a distance
of over 3,000 miles from where this seed was cast, Aimee Hope's
poetry has reassured me that the art spirit continues to pulse
toward the spirit of humanity.

And for that I am grateful.

> John Giarrizzo, painter and professor emeritus of art
> from Northwest College in Powell, Wyoming.

Some of us love the earth because we've been grounded by it.
Aimee's poetry is a testament to resilience and the art of turning
wounds into wisdom. Pain into beauty. Grit into diamonds.
Chaos into great dreams that refuse court orders and labyrinthian
borders and any more days free of bentonite between her toes…

> Tommy Gaffney, author *Whiskey Days* and *Three*
> *Beers from Oblivion*

Aimee's work isn't ordinary poetry. She takes you on an
emotional journey baring her teeth along with her soul, in what
sometimes feels against your will at gunpoint. Her essence
shines through: poetic, lyrical, dark, sexy, devastating.

> Justin Stubie Smith, author *Human Nature Walks*

Foul mouthed & accurate, Aimee Hope helps the reader get lost in a dense, visceral, visual confession; offering a sense of hope with biting sarcasm & wry humor. 'Held together by duct tape & bailing twine' she is still not backing down, still not giving up.

Dan Costello, Poet/Author

Feral Woman

Aimee Hope

Table of Contents

You're in Fucking Portland

Zombie-people posed like mannequins
in waxy flexibility,
hold cardboard signs on corners
of once-spirited, bustling streets
that vibrated with movement and life.

Ghosts have been replaced
by cockroaches and rats
scurrying behind plywood-boarded windows
and the fentanyl-addled
shuffle past deals made
in the open air.

Plexiglass boxes are screwed
into apartment hallways
housing two boxes of Narcan,
waiting patiently, stoically,
to squirt up the nostrils of the overdosed,
promising to try and hold someone
until maybe emergency services arrive.

Because mercury is in retrograde
and nobody really knows
what is in the latest batch
and your guess is as good as mine
whether an ambulance will show.

There is just not enough help
to hold this herd back:
the criminals know
the pens overflow
but the citizens still believe
this ain't no Mad Max shit

up in this bitch
where the only semblance of order
is the motorcycle cop in aviators
writing me a hands-free ticket
while a skeletal girl
with dirty, translucent skin
shoots up
on the sidewalk in front of me.

As long as we don't stare
at your emotional support stuffed animal;
don't rock this creaky, complacent boat,
we can pretend this shitshow
of a social experiment we call home
is not using human subjects
who never signed a release.

Authenticity

Authenticity is harder than I thought.
We are steeped in rules and roles:
fed Pop-Tarts, caramel coloring and Roundup,
waterboarded in Disney ears,
force-fed deception
down gullible throats
as we are fattened like duck
serving them up a foie gras
at dinner with corporate fascists
who control every aspect
of our lives
as if we are their property.
They tell you to hate yourself
and you buy their capsules and potions
and trick others into thinking
your genetic lottery
at least makes you a "6"
between goal posts that care more
about the car you drive
than whether you help old ladies
reach the dusty can of butter beans
in aisle 6
but you're at the end cap
and those Seen-On-TV gadgets
might change your life.

The Ocean

Bounce-walking at Kelly Point Park
like an ADHD annoying child,
I pick up rocks and shells
brought to gritty beach of Columbia
by persistent tiny, blue ripples.
You press them into palms
of potent hands,
telling me something feels magical
about this place,
closest to the Pacific
you can get in Portland.

We decide to skip the lake
and go to my place to fuck,
smoking that Crater Lake strain
I've been saving for you;
the smoke washing
a wave of desire
making me as wet as the ocean.

You tease me about my dry back porch
potted flower;
how it somehow bloomed
despite its dirt so parched
from my neglect.
Leaning forward in front of you,
my hip cocked,
I direct my ass toward your gaze,
exhaling delicate, sexy smoke,
connecting eyes.

Sometimes we fit together
like pieces of human puzzle
and tangle to grind
the terms of this endearment.
"I lost my mind coming here to have sex with you," he says
as he pats down his pockets,
looking for that black and mild sweet
he can never seem to find.

I come back to rock on deck,
stoned and drunk,
satisfied as we undress
so we can fuck a second time,
and I listen to you tell me
about a place on the Lake Michigan shoreline
you want to take me.

Postcards From The Highground

Wyoming dawn and I hear
the familiar metallic scrape
of the wood stove door swinging,
splintered wood thudding
against the ashy opening,
hinges quickly screeching,
dampening the roar and crackle
of burgeoning flames closed and locked,
promising warmth.
From my basement room
I hear the banked coal
igniting newspaper
printed with articles and your weekly column:
"Postcards From The Highground,"
promising to keep us warm
as I tuck blankets around my shoulders.
A whistling copper kettle whines
into the grinding motor
of a grimy overhead fan.
You cook conjoined link sausages
with a southwestern stamped fork,
paid for by words you wrote by the inch.
Five years after your body was found
crumpled in front of your door
and a message left by the coroner,
grief still marinated in heavy tears
and the realization that I don't let you slide
like tear-salty granules of sand
as the hourglass shattered.
I carry what I can of you,
the memories of horseback riding
on summer evenings,
the creak of the saddle,

self-sharpening wit.
I release you to the Wyoming wind
so it's no surprise you come to me in birds
gliding on that force
to be reckoned with.

Hummingbird

And just like that,
a blue-throated Mountain Gem
little hall-monitor,
try-hard flapping its wings
in my window
as I lay on my bed
in panties and a bra
to feel the cool fan blow,
contemplating the trees
just outside the window.
Black lab passed out cold.
Hummingbirds were my mother's favorite.
I watched her for decades,
make a simple syrup
she hung from plastic feeders,
back when red food coloring
was added into the concoction
that kept them buzzing back.
They scared me:
so sure of themselves
to move that fast.
How could they be so certain,
while I am trying to shake this funk
and be brave enough
to get my rice bowl outside
from the delivery driver?
How lazy I feel
in suspended animation;
as useless as Walt Disney's head
in some freezer warehouse.
I knew you for a moment
she whispered in my right ear
as if to say;

you don't have as much time
as you would like
and life is speeding by
so very fast,
like a hummingbird's wings.

Get up.

Fourth of July

Cars speeding by
on their way to next stop;
trucks shaking the bones
of this rented condo.
Snoring canines in front of my fan
while I remember blazing days
holding tiny fingers
to prevent scraped legs
from running in front of Shriner's turtle go-cart
or under impatient hooves of shod parade horse.

I wonder if I should have paused more
to take you all in at each age,
record more milestones;
take photos of it all,
to capture the wondrous joy:
ketchup, tears and spilled snow cones,
smell of gunpowder curling through blazing air.
Instead I wait alone:
for what? I don't know.

Empty nest sadness feels selfish.
It's hard to see forward,
when you made my past so beautiful.
All I can hear
are memories on repeat
and the goddamn Roomba
running into walls in the dark upstairs.

101 Degrees

Woke up early to beat the heat,
walking the path around the dog park,
caged teeth snarling through cyclone fencing
and we both know those dogs won't do shit.
Don't care anyway,
because my feet want to run
even though the fucked up
Jacque Cousteau scarring in my leg,
in my belly,
in my motherfucking brain,
tug and try their damnedest to leash me.

This bitch is done;
done with it all,
staining fuschia dye
into desert-dry hair.
I want to see that color
in the setting sun.
I create my own fucking world anymore.
People can be trusted
about as much as the fickle weather.
There ain't no weatherman alive
who can predict what the fuck I'll do next;
been running on survival instinct
for so long I don't know
how to sit on my heels
without overthinking.

Finding a pace
that isn't tugging on past trauma,
every beam of the desert sun
is like the supplication of opportunity.
Even if I fall on my ass

I will simply smile from the ruins
knowing I got back on the horse
that bucked me off.
I'm not at all who I thought I was.
There is no better place than the Vegas heat
to sort out what is what.

So, I give a nod to the vine shrub lady
shackled to chain link,
tethered by her roots
deep in the packed sand
doing can-can kicks,
her head tossed back,
headdress flowing in the morning breeze.

Asian women do a gentle exercise routine
in unison
on an empty basketball court
and I wouldn't fuck with them
or their tiny canine brigade.
Picking up the pace,
I decide fear no longer resides
at the core of this place inside
that wants to fight or freeze.
Everyone knows you can't freeze
when it's 101 degrees.

Willin'

Linda Ronstadt's sweet voice
and twangy guitars transported me
outside the damp, cracked basement walls;
an underground concrete prison.
Dusty pressboard turntable
the comforting hiss of the needle
feeling it's way through
a long, winding groove.
When will I be loved?
Good question, Linda;
and not one a child should have to ask.
She turned me out on parole;
transportation to the outside dimension
from concrete blocks,
the iron taste of the dirt floor on my tongue;
leading me to a sweet escape.

Linda was willin' to be moving
if she got weed, whites and wine
but I would pack my bags now
and learn to drive a tractor trailer
to take me far away from here
for the mere change of scenery
and to mute the shrill screech
of my name on lips
that shot verbal darts
and left raised red welts
still stinging half a century later.

Children love their mothers
even when they should not,
like the houseless man wears ripped clothes
because it's all he has;

all he knows;
and being covered in tatters
that smell something like you
is better than being naked.

We settle into what is comfortable;
what the usual is for us.
Comfort itself becomes a lie,
and you learn that Linda also knew
our hearts are like a wheel
that can't be mended when bent
as we keep rolling;
solid enough to move us along
wonky and wobbly;
but at least forward.

Faith can be clung to;
can be that lamp post in the storm;
a musty orange square of card stock
boasting "get out of jail free".
My captor changed the names of Boardwalk
and the city streets I longed for
to something small and local;
erasing the idea of the outside world
even on my Monopoly board.

Love was not free;
it was earned by saying the right thing,
wearing the right clothes,
being silent but pretty;
staying close to your vicious tongue
and his lingering eyes;
twitchy fists of a boxer
with hair ripped from my scalp
woven between his weathered fingers.

14

I sewed my own garments.
I bared my breasts to the sun,
defiantly.
I clung to hope
even if my faith dissolved to
leaving the darkness
to find any sort of light;
thumb up along the highway.
Linda taught me to love;
tracks of tears on my cheeks
as I clicked my heels and freed myself,
from this cage she named my life.

Clinging to her velvety textured voice
at the dark end of the street;
I felt like a pocket of dust,
and wind may carve holes in sandstone;
but a gust of wind cannot
keep you from blowing away.

That Bass

I was feeling kind of sad,
so I fucked the bass player (again),
long, thick hair still damp
under my curled fingertips
licking every inch
of pink slippery satin,
thighs pressed
against damp temples,
pumping Divine Feminine Energy
into his eager mouth,
later watching the same lips
smoke cigarettes on back deck
making small talk
as if we might hang out later.

Amplification

It's unfortunate
you may never see me stand
before a microphone
like a nine year old
on the edge of the high dive,
toes curled in discomfort,
eyes downcast
above a clear blue pool
smooth as polished glass.
There is no good way
to exit this plank of terror
without the fear of falling
through space and eyes.
The humiliation
of backing down those steps hovers:
once ascended,
there is no easy way down.

I'd rather fall to earth;
lips coolly suppressing words
meticulously chosen.
Let the insects clean my bones,
worms floss my eye sockets,
erase these words I've knitted together
with razor-sharp needles.
Let me decay then dig up my ribs
and use them in a voodoo ritual,
string my metatarsals in a garland
and contain my beating heart
in a dill pickle jar.

Standing in front of you,
baring my soul

feels worse than death.
It feels like over-exposure
and I might just stop breathing.
I would step over the edge
if I thought your snaps
could dampen the gleaming pain.
Vocal cords betray
feeling like dry chicken
from last Sunday's dinner
as I prepare to swan dive
into the judgment of strangers.

Birds of a Feather

She collects feathers
though she fears birds,
ever since that Alfred Hitchcock flick.
If enough are collected
maybe wings will fly her away
from here, to there,
where the wind blows
a little more gently.

She joins a Facebook group:
Dull Women of the Pacific Northwest.
Marie Lynn posted a rich bake
of tomato and high-spirited cheese,
perfectly tinged with brown bubble clusters.
A meal prepared for oneself,
with a rolled napkin of flatware,
Oneida, she guessed,
because it has some weight.
Rustic bread and fancy garnished butter,
prepared with such love and attention:
a "meal for one," Marie stated.
A meal prepared for someone loved.

Fingers shook as she typed,
and asked the woman
how she learned to love herself
enough to spoil with all the fixings.
The woman's reply was simple:
"first step was authenticity.
Then I started to like me better."

Her sharpest knife chosen
and cutting board open and ready,

she began to chop onions
(a good excuse for the tears)
dreaming of a dull life
with intention;
with hope;
with self-love.

there is blood.

"I was feeling really down," she said,
"so I fucked a bass player."
They laughed,
because she was the kind of woman
to do just that.
She could visualize this dark box,
full of secrets
that could only be released
by the sleight of hand.
Lying in her tub,
magnesium seeping through,
Fleetwood Mac strumming,
candle wick choking
on its own waxy vomit;
crackling to Mick Fleetwood's
meticulous beat,
when the only strength
to hold onto
is being one of The Seven Wonders
and knowing the pot
isn't full of gold.
Where there is gold,
there is blood.

Bryce Magic Hour

Glowing hues of pink, orange and red;
jutting castle spires drawn
to the azure heavens.
We stood before its majesty
as you searched for underground pyramids,
convinced this land is the true Holy Land.
How did your blind eyes take in the view
in the golden hour evening light
through glaucoma lens?

Two glorious weeks
soaking up your sweetness,
escorting through scorched sidewalks
to preserve your dignity,
my hand in yours guiding
so others couldn't perceive,
feeling personal failure
in Gucci flipflop scuffing curb.

Sometimes you're so hard
after being so soft
and the transition scares a girl like me.
I just want to melt into you.
You hold me back
and it hurts
because I just wanted to love you.
You've seen how broken I've become.
I need more.
No apologies needed.
Thinking of you
leaves me smiling
and aching- longing.

For now I try to snake my arm
through the maze of your limbs
to rest my head
against your warm, unyielding flesh
in the chill of spring Utah air,
as I cry the least tears
my guard will allow,
sliding down your arm
in this magic hour light.

Dear Frida,

I've stayed gone in my bathtub of tea
no stomach for hard liquor.
All the drawbridges
now rusted and jutting
into the sharp autumn air
beneath mold of moist leaves
now limp, yellowed and faded
like the memory of hot desert nights.
I still think of him
and hate myself for that.

New keys jingle
because changing locks
was not enough.
I moved far from any place
he can find me
(not that he is looking).
My heart cannot be trained;
it betrays me.
Snarling dogs guard my fence.
An orb weaver
has taken up residence
near the welcome mat
I've flipped upside down
inviting visitors
to leave well enough alone.

Please come to me,
but stay away.
My iron poster bed is in storage;
it calls to me,
while I spread Liquitex
on any canvas or wood

24

that will hear me out;
pages of verse stuck together
with tears from my eyes
he had no business invoking.
The cars go by
too fast to smell
the decaying stench;
rot from love-gone-sour
that poured one way
from my empty goblet.
He was hardly my Diego.

Midnight in Oklahoma

Billboard lights shut off on auto
Strawberry moon,
so full and bright and pretty.
She is charging moon water
and waiting for him to deliver her
some New Orleans cemetery dirt,
on his way back to his home
in the desert
where he knows his eyes
will get that light back.

He plunged his hand in an ant pile,
and still tried again
with raised welts on wrists
to retrieve the earth for me,
bringing it to me
in a crumpled Dorito bag
because I told him
I find the smell of the soil
intoxicating.

Phone went out in Tahlequah
before he left the Cherokee Nation.
He's gonna give himself an hour
to pull over and sleep
at a teepee-shaped gas station.

When he woke,
we laughed for nearly an hour
about a cellular double dog dare,
then talked some more
and some more
and then even more

about desert adventures,
unseen sights;
how I thought for a year
he liked to dress in women's clothing,
but really his Facebook was just hacked.

We laughed
and I can tell he smiles
during our calls
by the pitch of his voice.
He agrees I was born
in a midlife crisis
and our boundaries,
are both so fucking unhealthy,
but maybe between the two of us,
there is something whole,
and we can glue
each other back together.

We're In Vegas

"Because we're in Vegas,"
he said, "we can eat in bed."
And we did.
Backwoods honey blunts
and a little pinch me I must be dreaming
because you've been in my heart
and on my mind;
yet even in the desert sun
that warms deep into my marrow,
I wonder how I got here with you
because I pined for you
and cried when you left me on read.

You told me to get right
under the dry oven of heat
and afternoon naps;
hand-in-hand on blistering concrete.
You waited patiently while I balked;
wanting to run from the inevitable disaster:
hide my heart and tuck my tail
from my love/hate with people.

Yet I am learning to turn my back to yours
and know you will be there when I wake.
Mini Jolt speaker found your vibe.

Drain

Milky Way-smeared brilliance for miles;
gentle summer breeze cooling
sticky, starry, Montana night.
Sand rock bluff witness
to my Canadian visitor
who swears he cannot finish
in the presence
of another human.

Grasping the base of the matter,
eyes narrowed locking on his,
a lightly snaking tongue
tracing the underbelly,
sucking in breath
through teasing, flanged canines,
as if conserving the last morsel
of your air, of time, of your soul,
I might save for you.

I lean forward
and plunge my mouth
over your moral compass;
choking on the unsolicited tip
you almost offered;
your mouth now wide open
without finishing that thought
or having any hesitation
requiring your direction
as we edge on this ledge;
you're pouring any doubt
across the soft, pink tongue
as I swallow every drop,
then lie in wait like a sniper

to pre-order next week's supply.
Ragged breathing into Big Sky ceiling;
you slowly return to reality
and start singing,
"American woman!
Stay Away from me-eee!"
and my wet mouth
howls into the heavens.

Burn Notice

He just wants to put it all in the past
and label all the pain yesterday,
standing at the crossroads,
no devil,
no contract to sign,
no particular direction;
needle on compass spinning.

He doesn't care if it's his left
or right foot leading
as long as his feet carry him
the fuck out of here.
He travels miles
he hopes
he won't remember.

Calling me from the road,
he tells me violence is ill-advised
despite a face deserving
a little smack with my Jr. Slugger
"Get your hair did," he suggests,
"Put on a cute jacket,"
as I practice holding my head high:
feet don't fail me now.
Taking a crowbar
to loosen these lips pursed with fear;
he encourages me
to tell my harrowing story,
"then leave it on the floor.
Let the people slip on the blood
or tears or whatever,"
but don't burn this after reading.

Vacuum

I just want to curl up
in the crook of your arm
but you have shit to do
and we both know
that my heart has you in it
whether I like it or not
and maybe I'm not the kind of woman
you would bring home to your family,
but damnit we make a good team;
just like you said.

I'm a restless girl
but when you joked
about that Vegas chapel;
I'd be lying if I couldn't see
doing something crazy
and keeping it a secret
because the truth is
I don't want this to end;
I want to run away with you;
disappear into the desert.

You have felt like home
since that night on my deck
and I would drive all night
to lie on nails and tacks;
as long as it was with you.

So, I'll cry in the shower
and let the love seep from my eyes
because unrequited exists
only in a vacuum
and we both know I chase

what I can't have
and this is the honest truth.

I'll be fighting the urge to run
the looser you hold my body
because abandonment issues are a bitch
and I need a strong man to be patient.

I'm a good woman
who just wants to feel
the protection of your heart.
I've been banging on your door
until I gave up and pressed my back
to the splinters of your solid core.

I drove 14 hours
but my heart was behind the wheel
white-knuckling the asphalt path.
I'm right here in the Vegas sun,
and I accidentally packed my fear and loathing;
and we just don't make fucking sense
but I want to be near you now
and I don't want this to end.

Dark, Profane, Vulgar, Violent

Women speak through fingers
over screaming mouths,
vocal cords clipped
by male discomfort;
fingers that grip pens
with tense, white knuckles,
from twisted metal wreckage,
sharp edges slicing our limbs
when we speak of your free arms
with full range to strike,
to hold and control,
and silence.
You shield the pristine
with the protection of your fat wallet
and tell them bad things wouldn't happen
if I wasn't some sort of trash
to be tossed without a care
because I am your brother's refuse,
tossed out the window of a moving truck
after being raped and beaten
because *some women just deserve it*
and elevating their voice
turns your stomach.
As you see us coming with pitchforks,
are you quietly searching
your Rolodex of memories
in case a sharp tine
on the splintered handle
of vigilante justice
should bear your name.

Cunt

"Cunt," he called me.
"Angry, vulgar!"
(I've been called that twice
in two days.
Mental note:
mention to therapist).
My balking at meeting a man
I met online
who wants me to go to his house
"to cuddle"
because he wants "to lick
that pussy real good"
which for a minute,
short circuits my brain
and I tell him he isn't for me,
wish him well
but we all know
it won't stop there...
so I politely say goodbye
and admittedly laugh-emoji'd
his comments about my mental health,
how my boundaries proved me crazy,
my writing he never saw was terrible,
and the comment bubbles were boiling,
as he threw the grand finale mortar:
"I'm glad we didn't FUCK!"
#MeToo

Divebomb

Nose-to-ground
gives perspective;
there is nothing here to eat
but dirt.
My Dear voice actor,
knight with a pen sword
Rescue Ranger,
denim and tie-dye-clad
self-professed whiskey-loving slob:
we love the earth
because our noses
have been rubbed in it
for far too long.
We both want things
we know we can't have,
as someone snipped our strings;
the repair shop is closed.
We are problem-solvers
who need to quit
taking mouthfuls of soil.

At the end of the day
we must be asking for that shit,
and you are right
to tell me to take the blood
dripping from my heart
and paint a beautiful picture
because it's better than a mud pie

even though my grit
goes all the way down
between my teeth.
Pica is no regular diet.

Exodus

It's the day after pi day
and I'm drained.
We watched Shogun
and I felt kind of raw.
"I'm tired," I told him
and we joked that this is the day
I won't be passive-aggressively mean
and I admit he has grown on me.
He held back my hair
when I threw up Captain Morgan;
made me a chicken ginger rice congee
to soothe my burning stomach
and told me I create my own problems
(which I already knew),
so I offer popcorn, pussy and Pepsi
while rolling a joint of some indoor
homegrown shit;
with smoke rolling lackadaisically
to the sound of clanking katanas
and my lab's prancing feet
begging for a walk
to pee on the Visionary Park statue,
because nobody loves a colonist,
and Saturday is racing by.
I'm grasping at the door frame
of a place I desperately want to leave.

Feral Woman

Feral Woman looks out the window,
wind howling like a freight train,
pretending she is back in the woods,
steam of urine blowing toward her toes,
eyes scanning for predators.

Feral Woman peed in your boots
in a hot spring restroom
because your family eyeballed
her friend's black children;
Feral Woman made you stop and stare
squatting over fake Uggs
because it seemed the best place
for piss.

Feral Woman dreams
of shitting in your jack'o'lantern
and eats Taco Bell for days
in preparation.

Feral Woman sharpens her teeth
with the rasp of Dorothy Parker;
and smells of death and taxes.

Feral Woman is sometimes a sucker,
but she comes for you
in the dead of night
years later
with the verbal equivalent
of a sawed-off shotgun:
ask the woman in the fake Uggs.
Squish squish, Bitch.

Labyrinth

gravel crunching
     under Chaco soles
          ancestors urge me on

weeds tenaciously sprawl arms
     to the sparse Wyoming landscape
          like obnoxious noxious jokers

nausea erupts
     thinking of being in a womb
          of a woman who didn't want me at all

but I spiral inward
     warm morning sun
          on slumped shoulders

beaten the fuck up
     life like lyrics to a song
          but a country western one

the messages become more rapid
     more insistent
          as I find center

love with all your heart
     but you have to
          go your own way

all love has conditions
     except for the love
          you have for yourself

keep finding the center
     turn your face to the sun

people may be dicks
     but the Universe loves you

A Year Behind My 2015 Rav4

Spring

Behind my car
he lifted me
like Jennifer Gray
sliding down his body
to reality;
the true Wyoming Walkdown,
after he said I don't wanna be saved.
I love you slipped out,
flushed-cheek *I'm sorry.*
No you aren't. We both laughed.
Weeks go by,
resentment rising.
I gave up.
He missed me,
sent me Young Dolph's *Foreva,*
and called me Hope,
but said the *p* was silent.
I may be honorable,
but I'm not your whore.
Turns out he was blind
in every conceivable way.
My feet finally hit the ground.

Summer

Lifting black lab
boot of Toyota
Billy after Jo Armstrong.
Nimrod with cancerous
toe blueberry.
My legs wrapped his belly,

human cone of shame for weeks.
Toe amputation bandage unwrapped,
sobbing and begging,
bargaining with a god I didn't believe
for your life.
I can't live without you.
Your toe never touched the ground.

Fall

Hatchback rumble seat,
icy Coleman cooler ciders,
unseasonably warm autumn trails.
Hammering out enrollment
tattoo and hike club,
membership: 2.
Pushed me,
leapt down faith cliffs.
Only choice: climb up.
Return deposit on these bones
at empty trailhead.
Rock-wheeled roller skates
taught me to believe in self.
Hiking shoes grated into ground.

Winter

Truck headlight
puppet shadows
against Toyota backdrop.
Stammering like C-3PO
saying for hundredth time
he isn't coming on to me.
Daughters are a blessing
and I'm the daughter he has always wanted;
apologizing for wanting to spend

42

so much time with me.
Invites himself over to cuddle
when I told him I needed a nap.
I cry a little as I walk away,
because my boots are on the ground.

LOVEly FOOL

Eurythmics beat throbbing
preparing a rib eye
riding that pony;
tongue in teeth,
massaging spices seductively
in a sundress as brilliant
as the most glorious sunset.
She came to get down
she got off her seat
and jumped around
with a spatula mic,
damn skippy, baby.
With a simple salt and pepper
ready to sizzle on bars
she adds a little garlic
and maybe some onion pow pow powder
In the autumn afternoon
kids in schools.
She no longer fucks with
fall open houses.
and was never one
for the PTA
or making cupcakes
when she can serve that cake.
shaking that ass,
spitting lyrics in the air;
won't dance in public
but that kitchen
can be a scene.

Gyrating to Intergalactic
for no one but herself.
It's barely noon

44

and she has seduction on her lips
throwing it back and wagging those hips:
Here comes the hot stepper;
sheer panties straining
against her urge
to bust the foul meat
off her bones;
a little extra sass
for the one who thought
she was taken for a ride,
but who is the spider
and who is the web?
In the end it's all the same:
she is shaking that ass
to a fine 90's mix;
you gotta love yourself
cuz you'll always be there.
You are the desert
and the rain.
Keep feelin' love.

Painting By Letter

Painting by letter,
concise strokes outline the beauty
in that of which you do not consider,
but I dive to savor
the salty dirt and grit
from under bridges and toenails,
collect mental refuse
before sifting it
for something that clings
to my gnawing bones:
a sweet note from the mundane;
pursuing beauty in the repulsive.

Poetry is a phoenix rising
from an explosion of blood and guts.
The poet knows who and what to save
from the coals of disaster
by crafting something exquisite
in truth, ink scrawled on bar napkins,
stanzas on backs of energy bill envelopes;
drunken lines on a spiral notebook,
that may not ring any bells at dawn,
but channeling Horace
with words that are not mediocre;
intoxicated by the sky,
the wind blowing over the earth,
to feed you
a concise word sandwich;
ignite a candle to let burn
before walking away
to make of it what you will.
We comb the beaches
under the Hunter's Moon

for shining pieces of sea glass
made smooth from piercing shards
rolling in tumultuous tides,
strung with a simple truth
that cannot be unseen.

Because

Because at the end of the day
we are all just
the same reflection
of the best and worst
we thought of others
on our cloudiest days
and we all judge others
for sins we committed
at our worst.
You are right,
I'm a coward
hiding behind scorn
of anything that threatens me
with the nauseous pluck
from the pit in my stomach
that strums, "I am the Captain
who has been steering all along!"
It's best served with a drink
or the drug of your fancy.
I wish you the best
as we all just try
to figure this shit out.

Phoenix Claw

"You're the third woman
I've brought to dim sum
at this particular place,"
he said, smiling
into the sea of crisp white and gold linens,
clattering cups and plates.
A dishwasher roughhouses
with pots and pans
in the distant kitchen.

Hipsters nearby watch carefully,
obligatory Pacific Northwest beanies
hover above necks
clad in vintage Pendleton,
examining the morsels ordered
by my Chinese companion
from steaming, stainless carts;
hoping to "discover" the perfect bite
and go tell that
to their pretentious friends.

"I wouldn't tell women that," I said,
as he asked me to repeat myself
over the voices humming in the background.
"I thought dim sum was a dumpling," I said,
biting into a turnip cake;
confused that I was simply attending brunch.

He laughed and playfully said,
"you dumb Wyoming bitch,"
while offering me sticky rice
clinging to pork wrapped in a tea leaf
and a Phoenix claw,

exploding hot ginger soup
in my mouth;
touching the heart;
but not satiating
the appetite.

Wendover, Nevada

Your breath is slow and steady
as you stir in your sleep
when Pegaso comes seeping
through the hotel door.
Today we drive back
to our lives.
After three weeks together
I don't know how to walk
into the next room
knowing you won't be there.

But I will.

I love you.
You can deny it all you want.
I'm getting too old
to be with men
who don't know to choose me
and I'm learning to choose myself.

And I will.

You say you can't make me happy;
but you already have.
I want to be touched
and loved
and cherished.
I won't apologize for my desires
or water them down
to make them easier for you
to swallow.

And you do.

You say you sleep back turned away
and a moat of blankets between us
because you have a bad back
but I noticed your back is only happy
facing me when your breath slows
and all I want is to hold you
and feel the warmth of your body
since you deny my heart.

But you do.

If you can't meet me halfway,
I refuse to keep walking
the extra distance
while you decide
if I am what you want
but no matter what you decide,
I must choose myself.

And I will.

Reality Is Brutal

Gravitational pull;
stars orbit
centrifugal force
pulls tight;
gain strength;
imagine myself
tall as King Kong.
I pound my chest
while you beat
my drum.
Like a God.
I become icon.
My dear,
don't you know
this is an illusion.

"A Gift From Don Legg"

Sometimes the best gift
a man who touches little girls can give:
backward dive
into the cold clay
near a ditch
twisting bones
as the suicide gear teeth
engage to chew you up,
let the steel pads of the John Deere
grind your bones,
sort out your sins,
blending cerebellum and skull,
wedding ring pressed
like pie crust into your phalanges;
a blood bath of epic proportions
to be scooped up
by traumatized EMS workers
and you are thrown
in black plastic garbage bags
where you belong.

Daughters

How do I carry this burden
impregnated with venom and skeletons closeted,
gas that is lit by demons summoning
a stoic face I can't quite make
because I want to scream from a cliff
the things you said never happened.
My truth defies any wholesome landscape
you try to paint
but that isn't a scene anyone wants to experience,
so I cry alone on the toilet,
chest heaving in eruptions to the floor;
my rage too toxic for your virgin ears.
I have to pay a therapist
to listen to this shit
and it takes an entire session
to regurgitate my first memory
of what went horribly wrong
the first four years I can remember.

Is there such thing as low-key child sex trafficking
or is it normal for little girl aficionados
to have a wink-wink-nod-nod club
and a "your daughter should spend the night,"
because boys-will-be-boys
that turn into men-that-will-be-men
who think it's ok to ogle high school cheerleaders?
Their wives say nothing,
but make a hot Thermos of coffee
and shun the #MeToo movement.
Good wives *shut the fuck up*
and husbands tell them *you are too fat*
to keep them from thinking
they could stray;

with big booty porn glaring
from his Android hypocrisy
and the not-so-subliminal answer to every equation:
she will never measure up.

They drunkenly show their ball sack
to middle school boys on camping trips
with their buddies
and horrified reactions
are all they have to laugh about
while eating *The Fat Bitch's* Crock Pot cheese dip,
during super bowl commercials
and reminiscing about minors' thighs.

Your titillation has reached the station;
are you sure of your destination?

Your Creator knows you sit in church,
eat the body and drink the blood,
return to a home built by lies
where you have a daughter
you would protect
with your life.

Weapons

I sit in restaurants,
keep that back to the wall,
head on a swivel
and swivel and swivel...
keep my finger on your carotid,
press slightly hard
to remind you to keep that distance.

I listen with a little less judgment,
a lot more empathy,
an understanding of rainy days
spent staring at the wall
and the echoes of the creaking steel
that was my upbringing.
Connection is easy for me;
it's the abandonment of myself in that link
that will make me come for your throat later.

Yard tools have become weapons.
Fuck, everything is a weapon.
My tongue is a weapon,
forked and lascivious.

I give homeless people money
and goddamn it, I hope they buy liquor
because sometimes all we want is a party.
Gratitude overgrows in my garden.
I smile at passing dogs
and children and little old ladies.

Trauma informs me of any possible threat
as I crouch like a vicious tiger;
chips on my shoulders;

an attractive nuisance
ready to fight or flee
or fuck.

Crimes in Boxes

The fact of the matter
is nobody cares about him
or me.
People take sides because
the truth is so fucking complicated
and everything is a shade
from the charred remains
of heaven and earth
and Yin and Yang.

The truth is
there aren't many concrete things
to cling to in this lifetime.
Even science has more theories
than laws,
yet we put crimes in boxes
just like the people we don't understand.

His crimes will go unpunished.
I'm no one of importance.
I'm not worth the court time.
I'll always wonder
how I became a woman
who was afraid to call the police
on a man trying to kill me
because I ain't no snitch bitch
and I didn't want to be
the cause of some George Floyd disaster,
so I handled it myself,
the same way I handled it
before this brief intermission
(brought to you by

the pendulum swinging too far
in some fucked up direction).
When the courtroom door slammed shut
I learned that restraining orders
aren't made of Kevlar.
I'll always have to second-guess
a man who fooled me out of
choosing myself.

We are both still victims
of this ridiculous charade;
just cogs in a make-believe world.
At the end of the day we hold
the keys to a truth,
no one else could comprehend,
because that moment escaped
like the air from my lungs
when his hand held my life
between my mouth, nose
and the palm of his hand
as I fought for oxygen.
He was born with a grip
around his neck as well.
That's not my truth to tell.

Learn To Run

Your actions your own
and assaults like dot-to-dot;
marking path of destruction
on my head, shoulders, thighs;
not tracing an outline
of anything resembling me.
Make no mistake,
Calling me a "survivor"
Is the least offensive word
Merriam-Webster offers woman in these shoes,
who caught your hands.

Semantics won't provide the oxygen
you choked from my lungs
any more than quoting statistics
helped me feel safe enough
to ask for help:
5 pm always rolls around
and everyone goes home
leaving you on my doorstep,
blowing up my phone,
invoking terror
and some bullshit-trauma-bond pity
because you feast on my ability to love
and generosity of my human kindness.
Your strength is your weakness,
your anger a deadly weapon
(I didn't have it coming).
Maybe I couldn't fight back
in any meaningful way
but I took you down:
we're both on the right side of the bars.

I don't need your pity
because two of three of us,
(in any crowd)
statistically will experience violence
"but not me," you say;
(nervously looking around)
because women live with fear
most men cannot comprehend;
we live for so long seeking safety;
pushing it like an infant
in the seat of this cart that is our lives.
Walk in our shoes
and you will see
Why we learned to run.

Road Kill

Waking with a pit in my stomach
full of longing;
reaching for you.
You're a traffic light
giving me all the signals at once,
and I don't know whether
to stop
or go
or pause.

I know I need to change lanes,
but my hand is frozen over the turn signal
because I have no intention
of grinding the faucet down to a trickle,
even when I've flooded the basement.
I love with my whole heart
and it's bloody and beating
and bleeding out at your feet.

I just need to roll forward.
You just don't think about me
when I'm not around.
I listen to Bonnie Raitt
and wonder where along the route
of scorching Utah asphalt
I became road kill,
because I can't make you love me
if you don't.

Searching for Beauty

The Painter loves the form,
knows the drape of skin
from bones arranged
and still,
muscle as integumentary dress form,
in time-of-day lights,
The Painter describes in colors,
while Poet grasps for words,
ponders how and why,
of that which photos
cannot capture;
pens in hands that can't hold brush
to seek truth
of animal, vegetable, mineral.

Wet brush drawn,
in here and now,
where Poet fears
most to go;
won't look at own face,
where words can't describe
how it feels inside,
arranging loose flesh
from babies and illness,
unapologetically,
too many fucking tacos and tattoos.
Gravity pulls flesh to floor
like velvety theater curtain;
breasts hung low as drying orange in stocking,
thighs with folds
lover clutches
without promised disgust.
It's just sinew, tendon and Sephora.

She picks holes in face,
(mother says it's her ticket),
she destroys high-cheeked safety net,
(mother stated this negated need to change tire),
or alternative to education.
Picking way to truth,
paint tubes dried and portrait half-done.
Frida found freedom in her face.
The Poet's Nirvana is in there somewhere.
The Painter and The Poet,
both dusty miners of gold.
Each search for Beauty.

Acknowledgements

In 1991, I began my first semester at Northwest College in rural Wyoming, financed by a creative writing scholarship I won my senior year of high school at an on-campus writing event. This competition and Wyoming Young Author's program led me to identify myself as a serious poet and writer. After narrowly escaping a traumatic family life, I was uninspired and unsure of the trajectory of my 19 year-old life. During the course of a summer job bussing tables at Pahaska Teepee near the East Gate of Yellowstone Park, I met a young man who encouraged me to return to school and enroll in a course taught by his father, Burt Bradley.

Upon returning to school the next fall, I found Burt Bradley and his close friend, John Giarrizzo, to be a dynamic pair of young college professors who shook up a small, rural community college campus in northern Wyoming. Together, through art and literature, they taught students blinded by a conservative community, to see. With a twinkle in his mischievous blue eyes, Burt Bradley inspired me with his fearless passion for life, and ruined me for all the other men by stepping onto a chair in a sea of students leaving a basketball game to profess his love to his wife. Three decades later and three years following his death, I think of Burt Bradley every day and carry his poetry in my bag.

It was impossible to know I would find myself more than 30 years later, reaching out to John Giarrizzo to write a blurb for Feral Woman, when I found myself wishing Burt Bradley was alive to write it himself. I found John with his fist still in the air, declaring, "we must stand in the face of evil", feet firmly planted, with a glossy photo of Burt behind him on the wall over his shoulder. I am ever-grateful for the passion and wisdom I've garnered from these inspirational men, whose Art Spirit will always live on through their students. For that, and for the friendship and support for this book I have found in Burt's Brother, John Giarrizzo, I am grateful.

About the Author

Aimee Hope is a feral woman, artist and poet. Having spent her early years at her mother's feet on newsroom floors listening to the keys of typewriters and carriage release levers furiously clacking out stories; writing is in Hope's blood.

Growing up in rural Wyoming near Yellowstone Park, Hope was surrounded by inspiration of the beauty of the Rocky Mountains and the contrast of her liberal mother shaking up a conservative community. Hope took to writing on notebooks, napkins and scraps of paper to make sense of a tumultuous childhood. After attending her first year of college on a creative writing scholarship she won at a high school writing festival, Hope decided to attend nursing school and went on to own a healthcare business for over a decade. She never stopped writing. Hope's work has been published in various anthologies and publications over the years, but *Feral Woman* is her debut as a serious poet. After spending three decades working as a Registered Nurse, Hope has gathered her spunk and set out to show you how passionate and feral she really is.

www.ingramcontent.com/pod-product-compliance
Lightning Source LLC
Chambersburg PA
CBHW071216120626
46546CB00006B/2596